Pam plans a picnic

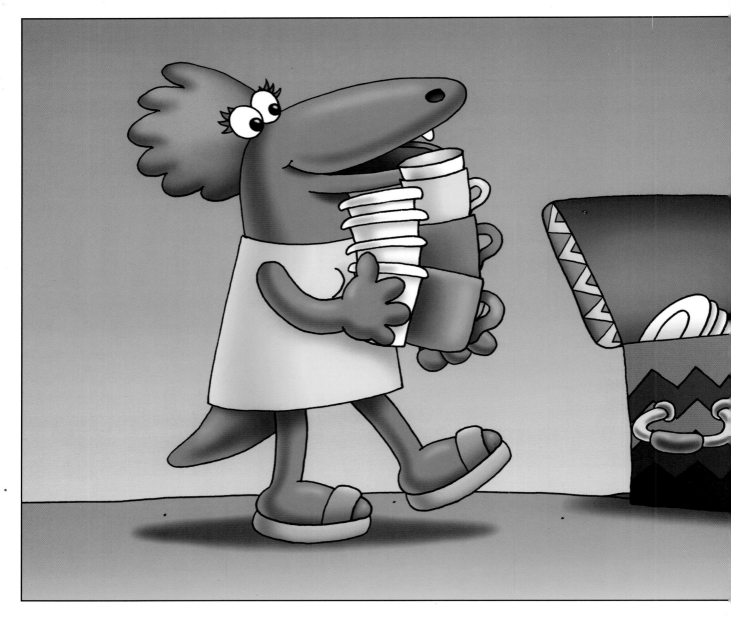

She packs a lot of stuff, and
Pip and Tim help.

She packs cups and mugs in a zigzag box, and mats and hats.

Tim packs a rug to sit on. It is big
and red and has lots of red fuzz.

Pip packs stacks of snacks in a bag.
It has a zebra print and a big zip.

Pip stuffs the bag with pots
and tins and pop and fizz.

But, at the picnic, the zip on the zebra bag gets stuck.

Sam picks up the bag...

... and Pam, Pip and Tim tug at the zip, but it is still stuck.

The bag rips!
The pop drops and the fizz pops.

Speaking and listening

Who are these characters?

Sam

Pam

Pip

Tim

Can you read these words?

van

yap

box

quack

Spelling and writing

Ask your child to blend and read the words below. Ask them to say each word and to tap out the phonemes (sounds) of the word with their fingers. Then ask your child to try writing each word.

jug

wet

lid

Understanding the story	These questions will help you to check that your child understands the story.

1 What is Pam planning? (page 1)

2 What does Tim pack? (page 4)

3 What does Pip put in the bag? (page 6)